Best of Friends

Carmel Reilly

Australia • Brazil • Japan • Korea • Mexico • Singapore • Spain • United Kingdom • United States

Best of Friends

Fast Forward
Green Level 13

Text: Carmel Reilly
Editor: Johanna Rohan
Designer: Vonda Pestana
Series Designer: James Lowe
Production controller: Emma Hayes
Photo Research: Corrina Tauschke
Audio recordings: Juliet Hill, Picture Start
Speakers: Matthew King and Abbe Holmes
Reprint: Jennifer Foo

Acknowledgements
The author and publisher would like to acknowledge permission to reproduce material from the following sources: Photographs by Alamy Images, p. 6; Getty Images/Jason Homa, p. 7 top/ Lisa Peardon, p. 4/ Picturenet, p. 5; Lindsay Edwards, front and back cover, contents page, p. 8, p. 9 top, pp. 10-24; Photolibrary.com/David Grossman, p. 7 bottom.

ISBN 978 0 17 012581 9
ISBN 978 0 17 012573 4 (set)

Cengage Learning Australia
Level 7, 80 Dorcas Street
South Melbourne, Victoria Australia 3205
Phone: 1300 790 853

Cengage Learning New Zealand
Unit 4B Rosedale Office Park
331 Rosedale Road, Albany, North Shore NZ 0632
Phone: 0800 449 725

For learning solutions, visit **cengage.com.au**

Printed in Australia by Ligare Pty Ltd
5 6 7 8 9 10 11 20 19 18 17 16

Evaluated in independent research by staff from the Department of Language, Literacy and Arts Education at the University of Melbourne.

Contents

Chapter 1

FRIENDS

Friends are people who are special to each other. Friends like to spend time together, and they have things in common.

Friends have strong **bonds** with each other. They share the good times and the bad times.

Some people have many friends.
Other people have just one or two friends.

Some people like to go out and do things with their friends!

Other people like to stay at home and have a quiet time with their friends.

There are many different kinds of people and many different kinds of friendships!

Chapter 2

JOSH AND ZAC

This is Josh and this is Zac.
They are best friends.

They have been friends since they were babies. This is because Zac's mum and Josh's mum have been friends for a very long time. They were friends even before the boys were born!

www.sportsco.com.au

Zac and Josh live near to each other.
They go to the same school,
and they are in the same class.

Running Words 155

Zac and Josh are there for each other all the time.

When Josh's dog was sick,
Zac went with Josh to visit him
at the vet's.

When Zac couldn't see a band
he really loved,
Josh got him a t-shirt and CD
– signed by the band!
SCORCHED
WHEELS &
DOLL BABY

Chapter 3

KATE AND JACK

Kate and Jack are good friends. They don't live near to each other and they don't go to the same school, but they share something else...

They both love basketball,
and they love to talk about it a lot!

Kate and Jack play basketball together every Saturday.
They also see each other at practice on Wednesday afternoons.

On the court, Kate is really good at shooting, and Jack is great on **defence**. They work well together in the team.

Chapter 4

MADDY AND MEI

Maddy and Mei have a different kind of friendship.
They don't even live in the same country!

Maddy lives in Australia,
and Mei lives in China.
They only see each other
when Mei comes to Australia for a holiday.

Most of the time, Maddy and Mei keep up their friendship by email.
They tell each other about their lives.

Maddy and Mei also like to send things to each other.
Mei sends Maddy pens, paper and notebooks from China.
Maddy sends Mei chocolate and books to read from Australia.

Chapter 5

HELPING EACH OTHER

There are many different kinds of friendship. Some people are friends because they spend a lot of time together.
Other people are friends because they have things in common.

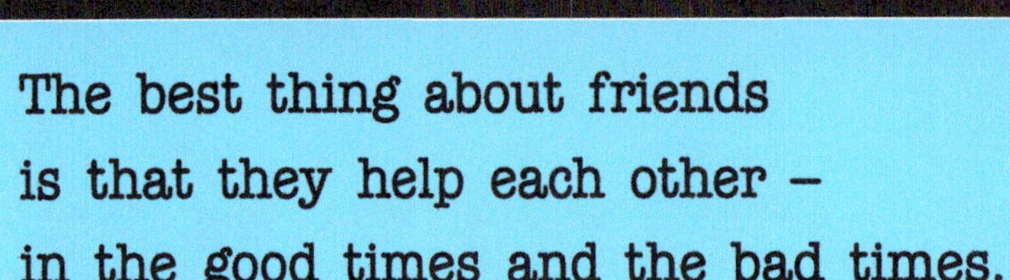

The best thing about friends is that they help each other – in the good times and the bad times.

Send Now
Send Later
Add Attachments
Signature
Options
From: Mei
To: Maddy
Cc:
Bcc:
Subject: Photos

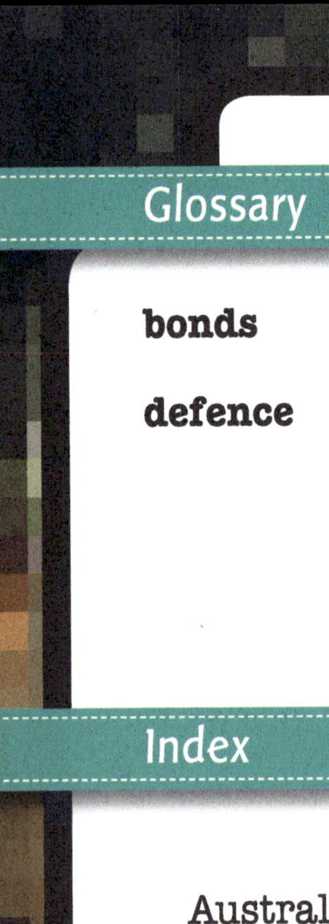

Glossary

bonds feelings that unite people

defence the role of protecting the ball

Index